NIGHTHAWKS

QUEER LOVE IN THE DARKNESS

NIGHTHAWKS

QUEER LOVE IN THE DARKNESS

MILES CIGOLLE

SUNSTONE
PRESS
SANTA FE

Sunstone books may be purchased for educational, business, or sales promotional use.
For information please write: Special Markets Department, Sunstone Press,
P.O. Box 2321, Santa Fe, New Mexico 87504-2321.
Printed on acid-free paper
⊗
eBook: 978-1-61139-778-9

LIBRARY OF CONGRESS CATALOGING IN PUBLICATION DATA

(ON FILE)

WWW.SUNSTONEPRESS.COM
SUNSTONE PRESS / POST OFFICE BOX 2321 / SANTA FE, NM 87504-2321 /USA
(505) 988-4418

FOR GORDON

PREFACE

It was the 1970s, the decade before AIDS hit, when gay men in NYC lost their inhibitions and discovered community on the dance floor and queer sex in the backrooms. Gay liberation was celebrated everywhere, especially after dark from West Village streetcorners to underground sex clubs, from 24/7 bathhouses to butch leather bars near the Hudson. These newly liberated men discovered queer sex outdoors in the moonlight, in the Ramble in Central Park or the Meat Rack on Fire Island, in the empty delivery trucks in the Meatpacking District or beneath the vaults of the Brooklyn Bridge. Each night the homosexual sissies donned their black leather or faded denim as they transformed themselves into nighthawks in pursuit of their next queer hookup. While the heteros slept peacefully in their safe suburban beds, we homos discovered the thrill of queer love in Manhattan's disco palaces, abandoned piers and subway tearooms. Join Miles on his nightly adventures exploring the City's shadows as he discovers welcoming community and the promise of forbidden love.

CONTENTS

1 / LOOKING FOR LOVE

1969. It was one year after the Stonewall riots; my first semester Freshman year at Cornell. I was still a pathetic virgin with only a few closeted friends. I was still a loner looking for a lover. That fall they gave us fags a Gay Dance in the main student union Willard Straight Hall. With a name like that I felt a little nervous. But I was impressed. They gave us the best room on campus, a soaring lounge that resembled the inside of a Gothic cathedral. But of course I spoke to no one. I just stared at the same-sex couples dancing slow, their hands on their boyfriend's pretty butts. I was jealous. When would I find my beloved? Nice attempt but no thanks, the dance mostly attracted lesbians. My only openly gay classmate Rich told me the real action was downstairs in the sub-subbasement. That's where Cornell's hottest tearoom was located. Rich was right about that but at the time I was too green for tearooms. They seemed awfully seedy. Instead I gravitated to Morrie's, Ithaca's only gay bar. Rich hung out there nightly. It turned gay after ten each evening. Before that it was totally straight. This meant I had to be a night owl. Prowling around in a dimly lit gay bar was definitely a step up. Was I now a nighthawk? Not yet by a longshot even though I foolishly went home with a pasty-faced grad student who fucked me up the ass. The creep didn't even bother to jerk me off. He hardly spoke a word. He just gave me my first case of gonorrhea. Plus I hated the stench of cigarette smoke on my clothes when I finally got back to my dorm room. None the less despite the humiliation I felt tremendous. I had finally come out, well sort of. I became a Morrie's regular. Rich eventually introduced me to the student union tearoom in the basement where a horny Senior knew just how to blow me. After a few months things were starting to pick up. I discovered Jim in Morrie's. Suddenly I was in love. Almost overnight Jim became my first boyfriend. Our mostly monogamous relationship lasted nearly a decade.

That first night Jim took me back to his basement apartment and butt fucked me in total darkness. The pain was excruciating. So I turned the tables on him. I started playing the top. It turned into our new playbook. Sucking, rimming, butt fucking. Jim was always the passive one. I was always the active one. I turned up the lights so I could see all the action. I installed sex mirrors by the sides of the bed. Our sex sessions were always hot and lengthy.

Within a few years Jim and I moved to Brooklyn Heights where the local piano bar on Montague Street put on drag shows. Jim enjoyed them but I just thought they were tacky. It wasn't until we moved to the other side of the East River into Manhattan and an artist's loft near City Hall that I finally discovered Gayville. That was Jim's name for the West Village. Hot gay men on the sidewalks looking for a casual afternoon hookup, their colored bandanas in a rear pocket proclaiming their sexual preference. Not just gay bars on every corner; there were also gay restaurants, gay bookstores, gay sex shops, 24/7 bath houses, everything a gay guy could possibly desire. Bars of all persuasions from fluffy piano bars serving gays in lavender cashmere sweaters to your butch leather bars for those into S&M fisting.

Of course Jim's favorite bar was Julius'; it was a gay institution. It's still at the same location located at the corner of Waverly Place and West 10th Street in the heart of the West Village. It's the oldest continuously operated bar in New York City. It turned into a gay bar in the 1960s. Jim loved the place—the sawdust on the floor, the green leather bars stools, the row of brass Dachshund boot-rests, the green glass lampshades over the bar that made the place feel cozy like an old collegiate library. The butch waiters were all super friendly in their black leather vests and spotless white tee's. It had three huge glass windows facing the street. That was unheard of at the time. Gay guys back then were sometimes afraid they'd be seen through a window in a gay bar and end up losing their job. That never happened at Julius'. Jim's favorite Saturday afternoon routine was popping in for his leisurely glass of red wine in a stem glass sitting comfortably in a window seat up front. From that vantage point he could take in the street life including his favorite gay bookshop across the street, Three Lives and Company. Julius' was a small place with lots of loyal regulars who all knew each other well. The long narrow front room had a tiny grill at one end for the best hamburgers and onion rings in the West Village. The one-man short-order chef was an adorable blond kid with a super-hot butt. Tony had a beautiful smile.

Julius' was popular with the mama's boys in their penny loafers and collegiate Ivy League sweaters. Jim fit right in. It wasn't a leather bar. That would have been too raw and sexy. It never had a backroom for anonymous sex though the toilet saw plenty of action. In the back next to the rear exit was a tiny quieter room with a few round tables if you wanted to have a private conversation. That room was painted flat black. Clientele signed their initials in white chalk on the walls. Newlyweds put their initials inside white hearts to look for decades later. When Jim and I split up, Jim's new boyfriend Philip kept up the tradition. He added 'Jimmy + Philip.' It was there even after they both died of AIDS. It always felt strange seeing it there as a reminder. Twenty years later on a return visit it was gone. Just as well; I needed to move on.

If you were like me with an interest in the kinky, the afterhours Hellfire Club in the Meatpacking District was your ticket. It featured guys into butch attire, real men with no attitude, like hot construction workers in muddy work boots, or firemen in rubber overalls, even NYPD cops in freshly ironed blue uniforms. The cops featured hand cuffs dangling from the hip. While Jim enjoyed the creature comforts of cozy Julius', I always opted for the kinkier scene at the Hellfire. Later on when I met Abbey we often dropped in just to see what was going on. Abbey was a member. It was in the basement of an abandoned five-story red-brick warehouse on West Street near the Hudson. Unlike the glass storefront of Julius', Hellfire was a hidden mystery. Its entrance was behind a solid unmarked black door. The building had boarded up windows. The door bouncer was dressed in leather but it was just an act. He was a sissy. Abbey knew him well. "Good evening boys. We're busy tonight. Officer O'Riley just checked in."

With that announcement I knew we were in luck. Inside the place was really hopping. The ground floor was a Latino disco which Abbey always enjoyed. The sex club was in the basement. That's where I spotted NYPD Officer O'Riley. He was in his official uniform. He saw me and waved me over. He was in character. Once he was inside the club he turned into a badass straight cop. "Hey cocksucker, get your butt over here boy. So I caught you sucking cock again on Christopher Street. You know that's illegal. I'm going to have to book you. Put your hands behind your back." I knew the routine. "Yes, Officer O'Riley." He cuffed me behind my back and forced me down on my knees. "Looks like you get to blow me tonight. You're lucky, I'm super-horny." Officer O'Riley pulled out his boner and forced it down my throat. I didn't complain. He had a beautiful Irish cock, nice and thick. So I gladly gave him his lengthy blowjob. He delivered a flood of thick Irish cum. Opening the cuffs to release me, he pulled out his citation pad from his back pocket. He made an official entry and handed me my copy. "Lewd behavior, Indecent exposure. Cocksucking." I was looking for love in all the wrong places. I was young.

2 / BOMBER JACKET

When Jim's Princeton buddy Gordon showed up unannounced in New York City near the end of our nine-year relationship, I knew we were in good hands. Gordon always projected an air of casual queer sex. I thought he was a sex master. Maybe he could teach me something. My sex life with Jim was so boring. Gorden showed up in his olive-colored bomber jacket. The one with the orange inside liner. It showed off his cute butt and his plump crotch. It was the bomber jacket street hustlers used to wear with button-fly Levi's, white sneakers and a tight-fitting white Calvin Klein tee. Gordon really dressed like a street hustler. I often wondered if he didn't hustle on the side. He was very private about his sex life. Once I overheard him confess to Jim that he was a top and that he loved to fuck young guys while wearing his bomber jacket. I immediately loved the fantasy. I dreamed of doing just that for years. But in my version I was the one wearing the bomber jacket and Gordon was the one getting fucked.

On this year's annual visit to New York City, Gordon immediately announced he was taking me to the Eagle in the Meatpacking District on Saturday night. It was his favorite butch hangout. "The kid needs an education. He needs to experience a real leather bar." Jim agreed, no questions asked. Gordon was keen on showing me the infamous backroom at the Eagle, that raunchy sex den with uninhibited queer leathermen. Gordon told me I could borrow his black leather chaps to wear over my Levi's. I always dreamed of getting fucked in chaps.

15

I'd never been inside the Eagle. In fact I'd never even been in the Meatpacking District at night. My heart was pounding as Gordon opened an unmarked black door. Gordon knew the bouncer well. Inside the strong scent of poppers was overwhelming. My head was instantly numb. I could make out half a dozen bikers posing at the bar. Most were dressed in leather head-to-toe. Gordon bought me a beer and introduced me to a German biker couple named Hans and Otto. Gordon mentioned they were gay twins. When I jokingly asked if they were into threesomes, they straightened me out real fast. "Don't knock it 'til you've tried it boy." I turned beet red. "Sorry, no offense intended. I'd love to try it out if you'd like to play my masters. I'd gladly be your slave." "You bet boy." Without speaking another word they ushered me into the sex den.

The aroma of poppers in the backroom was much stronger. My head was high in an instant. My eyes gradually adjusted to the darkness. The backroom was dimly lit by exposed red ceiling lights. I could make out a guy in a harness who was butt fucking a hot Porto Rican kid with a dog collar around his neck. I quickly realized I'd made a big mistake. But it was too late, Hans had already ripped open my fly and taken my hardon into his mouth. His fleshy tongue was warm and wet. I played with his thick moustache. What a thrill as my cock slid past the saliva drenched hairs, my fingers inside his mouth.

I felt a warm wet sensation in my exposed butt crack next to Gordon's chaps. It was extremely pleasant. Otto was busy running his tongue up my buttocks licking the deep crack, rimming the tender anus. He licked the anal membrane with the tip of his tongue, drenching it in his thick saliva. Once Otto had my butt properly primed, I heard him put on a condom with a loud snap. One pass of the KY tube across the entire length of his cock, then he slowly fed it up my ass in one unbroken movement.

After a long pause, I slowly relaxed. The pain eventually passed; I landed in queer heaven. The two German twins serviced me well, one oral, one anal. I was completely satisfied. I reminded myself to thank Gordon. I was finally gaining some real sexual experience, the first in a long time. It marked my first threesome with me in the middle getting fucked and blown at the same time.

Hans and Otto started to part company when I reeled them in for a group hug. Hans spoke up first. "You sure have a beautiful cock. I'd blow you again anytime." "Thanks a lot Hans, you are a master cocksucker. And Otto fucks like a horny teenager. You know, that was my first threesome. Let me buy you both beers. This was my first time in the backroom of the Eagle." "Congratulations Miles. You handled it like a stud."

My first night at the Eagle changed everything. The taxi ride downtown to our loft was in silence. Jim, Gordon and I hardly spoke a word. We all knew I would never be the same. My initiation as a queer adult man was a success. My gay adolescence was over. My relationship with Jim would be finished within a month. He would always remain a close friend and a father figure, but never a lover. Gordon became a new sex buddy. Now on his annual visits to New York City I could trade places and show him the latest gay discos, leather bars and underground sex clubs. His favorite was The Saint. He loved the music, the dancing and the hot men; but mostly he loved the balcony sex. Gordon was a lot like me.

3 / BLACKOUT

It was the summer of the New York City blackout. Our first summer in Brooklyn Heights. It was brutally hot. Jim was in Vancouver visiting his parents. I never went with him. He's not even out to his parents yet. Isn't that pathetic? The blackout meant the subways were out of service, so my office was closed. I was stuck at home in the hot apartment with no air conditioning. I was getting sweaty. I headed to the Brooklyn Heights Promenade to cool off, escape the heat, maybe do a little cruising. I dressed for the occasion in my raunchy Levi cutoffs, an old New York Yankees tank top and my old sneakers, super-casual and sexy. Underneath the ripped cutoffs I chose an old jockstrap. You could see it bulging out a bit through the torn cutoffs. The look was super-raunchy. Sometimes I like playing the slut.

The promenade was quiet. I had a wooden bench to myself near the north end not far from the public toilets. It was a gay tearoom that saw a lot of local action. Not for me that night. It was too early and besides I was way too sweaty. It must have been near a hundred degrees. The view across the East River to Lower Manhattan was hazy. The air was still and sultry. I heard a loud squeak from the door into the men's public toilet. It needed oil. Out stepped an overdressed gentleman, in Ralph Lauren head to toe. A grand queen, complete with the ascot and Gucci loafers. How he could tolerate the extreme heat in such an elaborate costume was amazing. I nodded, waved him over and gave him a friendly smile.

19

"So how were the toilets?" He blushed red. "Sorry, that was rude. I was just having a little fun with you. I go to the toilets myself all the time. Hello, my name is Miles. I live nearby on Remsen Street. Isn't this heat brutal?" "As bad as London in July. Indeed it's hot. The tearoom was empty. Only the emergency battery light was working. After fifteen minutes I gave up. I'm getting too old for this don't you think?" He chuckled. "Good evening. I'm Michael." The elderly gentleman sat down next to me. His voice was soft and gentle. I liked him immediately. I thought I ought to give him a hug, but I held back. I didn't want to scare him away. "Shall we go for a stroll? There's the illusion of a breeze when you're walking."

That's how we met. Michael was refreshingly candid. When I asked him what brought him to Brooklyn Heights his answer was insightful. "Why the cock of course. New York City men all have big cocks don't you think? Much better than those puny ones back in England." He made me laugh. During our leisurely stroll I made sure we ended up in front of my brownstone. I pointed up to the top floor windows. "That's where we live. My lover Jim is away. Could I entice you up for a lukewarm Pellegrino?" "Absolutely young man. Maybe I could get inside your American "cutoffs" as you call them. You don't see anything like those back in London."

That's how it all started. Michael announced he was strictly a bottom. He slowly pulled off my jockstrap just using his teeth. He was an expert cocksucker. He knew just how to drive me crazy. Michael was really into cum. He swallowed every drop. He prefers American to English cum. He told me American cum is much sweeter. He made me feel like a prince. We talked for hours in the living room on pillows on the floor as the sky darkened. It turned out Michael lived in a renovated carriage house on Cranberry Street just a few blocks away. His Black lover Zack was a banker in Lower Manhattan. That's how they ended up living in Brooklyn Heights.

Then Michael dropped a bombshell. He told me Zack was his S&M lover. Zack was Michael's butch master. Michael was Zack's obedient slave. Zack was always on the lookout for fresh meat to form a threesome to spice up their sex life. Michael thought I'd be the perfect fit. Of course I was immediately turned on by the idea. I'm such a slut. I'm always turned on by a little kinky S&M sex. That was about the time the power was finally restored. Michael called up Zack. The plan for our evening threesome was set.

We picked up Chinese takeout from Michael's favorite on Montague Street and headed over to the carriage house to meet Zack. He was an Adonis in black Levi's with a studded leather harness over his muscular chest. He was a real hunk. He smiled as he stared at my cutoffs. "Welcome, welcome. What a beautiful butt. You did real good Michael." Clearly this was a routine. "Thank God the power is back on. Let's all just strip down and get well acquainted. Miles you look super-hot. How about a little S&M sex; nothing too heavy? I understand you've already met Michael. He's my sweetheart." I gave them both warm hugs. Of course Zack took charge. He liked to play the master. I was happy to be his butt boy. He soon had his hand in my butt crack. "Very nice Miles. Let's just sandwich you here in the middle between Michael and me. We'll take you for a ride." Zack fucked me to his heart's content while standing tight behind me. I must have really turned him on. Up front, Michael gave me another round of perfect head, even better than the first one I'd enjoyed in my apartment. I was the lucky guy in the middle. After a long sweaty session, we showered out back in their garden deck.

That's how I met Michael and Zack. Later on Michael told me he had his eye on me from the moment he stepped out of the promenade tearoom. He already knew where I lived. He'd followed me home from the promenade weeks ago. He'd already had his eye on my butt in the raunchy cutoffs. He'd orchestrated the whole thing. He knew Zack would want to fuck me. I guess I should thank God for those old cutoffs. They're truly electric. I decided right then and there that I'd ask to be buried in them. Wouldn't that be a hoot?

My encounter with Michael and Zack was the highpoint of that special summer, the summer New York City had its famous blackout. That blackout was a once in a lifetime event. It never happened again. I was in my youth back then, always looking for a queer adventure. All us queers made the most of the blackout. Guys have tales of kinky sex from that night. Butt fucks inside stalled elevators, blowjobs in the dark on the promenade, even an out-of-control gay orgy in the subway tearoom at the St. George. But our Cranberry Street threesome was not to be repeated. I never told Jim. But later on I gave Abbey every detail, including Michael's English jokes and a detailed description of Zack's gorgeous Black cock. Abbey understood. We were all brothers in our youth, living life fully for a single day, for a single night.

4 / DANNY BOY

Sheridan Square at midnight. It's a week before Christmas. It's snowing lightly. The Christmas tree lot on the corner of 7th Avenue is closing down for the night. The smell of cut pine trees is strong, full of childhood memories. Childhood is a distant dream. I'm in another universe here. This is a world of queer men and queer sex. Christopher Street is deserted except for a few street hustlers posing in the doorways. I'm headed west toward the Hudson past the shuttered storefronts. My teeth are chattering out of control. It's a combination of the cold wind off the river and my nervous anticipation. I'm headed to the Christopher Street Bookshop on the corner of West Street; the infamous sex shop with the backroom where gay men gather on snowy nights like this. I haven't been here for several months. I always wear my leather motorcycle jacket and my old button-fly Levi's. Bob told me it's always crowded when it snows. The snow brings out the faggots for some reason. Perhaps because it makes us think of Christmas. I'm walking fast. I'm already half way there. My teeth are still chattering. I feel my heart pounding. I cross paths with a cute dogwalker. He smiles checking me out. I nod. I look back. He's stopped, waiting for me. He's hot. I hesitate for a few long seconds, then I turn back and resume my walk towards the Hudson. I must stay focused. My teeth are still chattering. The sex shop awaits me on the corner. The sexual attraction is overwhelming.

I'm shaking as I turn the door handle; it's pleasantly warm inside. The immediate heavy smell of poppers makes my head numb, calming my raw nerves. The leatherman attendant nods welcoming me inside. A leather couple is busy looking at the glass display case of sex toys. The tall one takes

23

out a large black dildo examining it carefully. He fondles it slowly, every realistic detail of the cock head, every soft fold of the glans, every raised vein on the shaft and then to my utter astonishment he suddenly swallows it whole deep down his throat. He sucks hard on the entire length of the dildo as the attendant looks on in approval. He works the frenulum with the tip of his tongue, licking it over and over. Finally he pulls the dildo out. He looks extremely pleased. The short one pays and the couple leaves together with the dildo in a brown bag.

The vintage subway turnstile beckons me into the dimly lit backroom. I've been here before. I can see half a dozen men inside cruising under the red lamps. A biker is posing against the brick wall. His knee is raised. His black leather jacket is old and well worn, dull and faded. I'm definitely interested in him, I'm ready to enter at long last. My teeth have finally stopped chattering. I hear the tiny bell as I pass through the turnstile into a pool of darkness. I feel a hand on my crotch. I brush it aside. It's too early for sex. First I want to enjoy the hunt. In the darkness I can hear the sharp sound of raw flesh being slapped by bare hands. I feel hands on my button-fly, then a wet moustache around my cock, a powerful tongue, a flood of warm saliva. I give in. It's too inviting to refuse. I feed my cock past his moustache deep down his throat. I rub his smooth bald head. He swallows even deeper. I massage his wet moustache. I'm in heaven. But it's much too soon to cum. I've only just arrived. I kiss his bald head before returning to the hunt. I pull out, back into the shadows. My eyes slowly adjust to the darkness.

Men in motorcycle boots and jockstraps giving blowjobs to college boys in sneakers and sweaters. I'm more interested in the biker I saw near the entrance in his worn studded leather jacket. He sees me staring. He turns to adjust his cock for me; it's straining against skin-tight leather pants. The biker hands me his open popper bottle. My head explodes. He hands me his cock. I take it all in. It's perfect; but not yet. It's too soon. The biker and his beautiful cock must wait. I recede back into the shadows.

The Christopher Street backroom is too warm. They keep it toasty for us faggots. They also keep it stocked with plenty of cock from the muscle boys.

24

That's what I'm checking out now. Butch men with hardons looking for some rough action, not romance; perhaps an intense blowjob, a quick butt fuck, a smooth circle jerk, maybe something a little kinky. Perhaps a queer threesome. Anything is possible here. I'll hang out in the shadows, in a dark corner. I'm in no hurry. I'm enjoying the show. I'm looking for something special, something a little different, something that I'll remember on the subway ride home later.

My hesitation has made my biker bolder. He disappears into the shadows following me. He yanks on my jeans forcing them down with both hands. Without hesitating he works a fresh wad of saliva into my butt crack, rimming my tender anus. It's thrilling; but sorry, it's still too soon. I pull away again buttoning the Levi's. I retreat again into the shadows. He follows again; this time he kneels in adulation as I open my fly for him. Looking up he speaks for the first time. "You like to play hard to get. Let's go for a ride on my Harley." He smiles for the first time winning me over instantly. "You're quite the stud." His name is Danny. We get on his Harley. I'm seated on back with my arms around his muscular torso, my nose in his thick black hair. The cool night air feels good. Danny takes us to the empty delivery trucks in the Meatpacking District. Our sex is rough and kinky. I make sure Danny is satisfied. Afterwards he wants to blow me. I shoot my fresh jism on his black motorcycle boots. He works the warm cum into the leather with his bandana. It leaves the leather soft and shiny. He smiles. "I see you like that." "You bet I do."

We had breakfast at the Empire Diner. We were the only ones there at that hour. Danny was completely famished. After pancakes I told him a few dirty jokes to get him laughing. He had a beautiful smile. Danny was definitely Drummer material, a super-hot sexy stud; but he was also so shy and quiet. A real sweetheart. I fell for him in an instant. We traded phone numbers. "Goodnight Danny Boy, you're gorgeous. You can fuck me again anytime anywhere." "Really? I may give you a call. You were terrific. I like you."

What a surprise. Usually I hook up with butch older guys. I actually prefer older men who have their act together around queer sex. They don't have to prove anything like a lot of the young hot shots on Grindr. They're egoless.

Danny was just a young kid. Most young gay guys are a mess, but Danny was a little different. He was a sensitive guy. A beautiful gentle soul. I wanted to help him out. Give him a hand up. I didn't want Danny to have to go through everything I did. I put his number in my "trick box" on the desk. Maybe next time it snows lightly at night I'll give sweet Danny a call. Maybe we could share a romantic candle-lit dinner out in the West Village somewhere. Put the sex in the empty meatpacking trucks on the back burner. Instead maybe a slow massage in my bed. See if my darling Danny Boy is ready for true love.

5 / Monte Caprino

I was in luck. The garden gate was still open. It was 1:45 am. The place is full of queer history. Centuries of queer cruising have been recorded here. I bet Michelangelo cruised here overlooking the Roman Forum. The steep hillside was just a short walk from Rome's Campidoglio, the historic center of the city shaped by Michelangelo himself. In ancient Rome traitors who were condemned to death were flung from the adjacent Tarpeian Rock. For centuries the steep hillside was used for grazing sheep and goats. In the 15th century it became an urban garden, one of few in the congested inner city. But its rough terrain with its twisting staircases and ancient overgrowth made it unusable for proper ladies and gentlemen. That's when the queers discovered it. It suited our prerequisites perfectly; it was hidden and ambiguous, full of mystery and danger. Its steep rocky slope was conducive for queer cruising, for communal gay sex out in the open. It soon became Rome's most notorious gay cruising grounds, active late into the night. It was thought to be dangerous after dark. Crimes were not reported; murders were covered up. The sense of danger only added to the illicit sexual attraction. Queer cock was always available with quick one-on-one hookups, even small group orgies into the wee hours. At sunset the gates were locked except for one at the southernmost edge. Rumor had it that for decades Rome's queer police chief fucked boys here late into the night. When he passed away the city fathers thought it wisest to give the faggots a garden of their own since it would keep them out of public sight. And it did. It soon became known world-wide that Monte Caprino welcomed homosexuals from across the globe. It had an international clientele. Strolling through the garden on a summer's night one heard men whispering in foreign tongues. Looking closely in the shadows one saw cocks of all races, shapes and sizes.

I smiled. Thank God the garden gate was open. I was greeted by a butch body builder named Maximus. He was the official lookout. Maximus maintained the order. Everyone loved Maximus. "Welcome Gent, where are you from?" No one in Rome had a clue where Albuquerque was, so I always just answered Chicago. That way they wouldn't freak out. Tonight seemed on the quiet side. A couple in the bushes just off the main path were preoccupied with their trousers on the ground. They didn't seem to mind in the least bit if I watched. The kneeling guy was rimming his partner as he slapped his fleshy butt. It was already rosy red.

Up ahead I saw my friend Francis sitting on a wooden park bench. He waved me over. I sat down next to him. Francis was the in-house gay priest from nearby Santa Maria in Cosmedin. The 8th century church is famous for the so-called "Mouth of Truth" a large ten-foot marble disc on display in the front porch representing a human face. Legend has it that the mouth will close on the hand of any perjurer who places his hand there. Gregory Peck and Audrey Hepburn had a famous scene here from the movie Roman Holiday.

Francis showed up here most nights seated on his bench in his black robes and white collar. The bench practically had his name on it. He knew everybody intimately. I preferred to sit down next to him so he could fondle my cock through the soft denim. He liked that. He always made me hard. Francis would indulge me and give me head. We never minded the onlookers. I would just unbutton my fly, lean back and close my eyes. Francis knew exactly what I liked. He was a master cocksucker.

From our bench perch we could see the couple I saw earlier on the way in. They had progressed from oral to anal. The guy who was doing the rimming was now standing tall while butt fucking his partner up the ass. They were both young and athletic. It looked awfully hot. I envied the tall guy doing the fucking; he had an enormous cock. They were standing under one of

28

the few street lamps, so I could easily see the guy's giant brown cock. It was wet and shiny from plenty of lube. Francis told me he knew the guys. They were a leather couple who regularly attended Sunday Mass at Santa Maria in Cosmedin. They came here often looking for a threesome. Actually Francis knew many of the regulars here. He was their confessor. His bench was his confessional. He was often approached by practicing queer Catholics seeking his blessing and eternal forgiveness. The poor conflicted faggots suffered from years of Catholic guilt.

On my way out I spotted a biker dressed in leather posing next to a massive tree trunk. He was definitely my ticket. He seemed interested. He motioned me over with a silent gesture. Sure enough, his hand was soon inside my Levi's, his finger in my butt crack. He knew what he wanted. "Show me your butt." I opened my fly for him dropping my jeans to the ground. He fingered my butt crack. He spit out a huge wad of saliva sliding his middle finger deep up my anus. This was exactly what I craved. "Go ahead stud, fuck me. Use a condom." He had a slow fuse; he took his time. He butt-fucked me tight against the tree trunk. He spared me nothing. I took in his passionate lust. We climaxed a sea of cum together.

Seeking a respite the biker and I walked over to the Campidoglio. I wanted to show him Michelangelo's superb architecture, Rome's most beautiful outdoor room. I showed him the famous arcades lined with the rows of tall columns, their obvious reference to male erections. My biker was duly impressed. We set up an afternoon date for tomorrow to tour the Capitoline Museum. I showed him the bronze bust of Michelangelo and the nude marble statue of his beloved teenage butt boy Cecchino dei Bracci. We closed the museum. It was already getting dark. "Let's check out Monte Caprino." We returned to the scene of last night's encounter. I asked my biker to strip down to his leather chaps and hug the ancient tree trunk. He knew exactly where I was headed. I fucked him hard up his butt tight against the tree; first he moaned out loudly. Then I fucked him even harder in total silence. His beautiful butt was all mine. I slapped the soft cheeks hard with my bare hands turning them red and numb. We were two satiated lovers reclaiming Rome's oldest queer garden, this time in honor of Michelangelo himself. I felt the approval of the ghost of the genius; he still haunts Monte Caprino each night.

6 / Until Sunrise

The International Stud was world famous for its backroom with insatiable cocksuckers. It was a favorite hangout for wannabe leathermen and mama's boys like me, the Brooks Brothers and Ralph Lauren sets. Those were the butch sissies who liked to suck pretty cock in the dark after dinner, like a dessert, plain and simple. Weekends The Stud packed in the horny young faggots kneeling on the floor in their chinos praying at the altar of cock. The plain front door on the sidewalk was unmarked; it was only for those faggots in the know. On my maiden voyage two different strangers blew me, a hot young Puerto Rican kid and a much older super-butch leatherman. They were both fantastic lovers; they were both a little kinky. Needless to say, I had a wonderful time.

The front room with the zinc bar was small, practically cozy, the sort of room that feels like a club. The guys were friendly and casual. Nothing prepared you for the larger backroom. The steady stream of queers who entered it were silent, as if they were filing into Sunday Mass.

Plunged into darkness, I soon felt some guy's hands on my belt pulling my Levi's down to the floor. His powerful tongue started licking my jockstrap until it was dripping wet with saliva. I pulled the strap down for him so he could give me a proper blowjob. He took my hardon deep in his throat easily swallowing it whole. Soon I was rock hard. He handed me an open popper

31

bottle. I took one hit, my head exploded. Leaning back against a wall I settled in for the duration. I half closed my eyes. He worked the shaft like a pro, then the glans. But his real interest was the frenulum, that special tip of the male sex organ that drives us gay guys crazy. Each sensitive fold, each deep recess, taking his time, licking it slowly with the tip of his tongue over and over. He didn't let up. Working the frenulum he could taste the pre-cum. This guy was really into it. I opened my eyes to look at his face. He was a leatherman. He had a shiny bald head and a bushy black mustache. We made eye contact. He was gorgeous with jade green eyes; dressed in worn leather head to toe. He held my torso tight with both of his hands. He demanded total control. He continued licking the frenulum tip, now even more slowly with the very end of his long-pointed tongue. My whole body spasmed as my cock exploded wads of cum in generous bursts. He drained me completely. I was exhausted. I kissed his bald head. The feast was suddenly over. Apparently this was all my stud had come for. He was a man of few words. I smiled and hugged him. He retreated into the darkness. I already missed his powerful tongue, his shiny bald head, his wet black moustache, his beautiful jade green eyes.

I needed a break. I pulled up my jockstrap and Levi's, then headed for the bar up front. A few bikers were talking at the bar. The tall skinny one was extremely hot in his ripped Levi's. He looked like Peter Fonda. He saw me staring at his crotch. He gave me a friendly nod. I took that as a good sign. I caught him checking out my backside. Then he walked over and smiled. "Come here often? Enjoy the backroom. Maybe I'll catch you later. You have a hot butt, a James Dean butt. Be careful in the backroom; somebody might try to rape you." I blushed. I'd never encountered anyone so direct around sex. It was thrilling. "Thanks for the tip. Maybe I'll see you later. I'm Miles." "I sure hope so. I'm Tom."

Pleased with the sudden turn of events, I returned to the backroom to consider my options. Instead I noticed a red glow of soft light shining across the ceiling. The source of the light were the two emergency-exit lights over the doors at the front and the rear. Flesh turned a warm reddish hue as if lit from a winter's bonfire. Only the guys standing directly under the exit signs were clearly illuminated. This was where I watched guys getting special blowjobs.

32

Mindful of the biker's tip concerning the safety of my butt, I stood leaning against the wall. I closed my eyes and listened to men sucking cock. The stillness was punctuated by the sharp pops from the sound of some guy getting a passionate spanking. With each loud slap on his butt he let out a soft audible moan.

Soon I felt a hand on my belt, then on my button fly. Pulling my jockstrap down he instantly devoured my cock whole. I kept my eyes closed as his warm powerful tongue licked the shaft with full force. It felt tremendous. I opened my eyes. I discovered a bare-chested kid in running shorts kneeling at my feet. His head was shaved to create a classic mohawk haircut. The black hair of his mane was waxed tall and thick; I found it extremely erotic. The movements of his blowjob accentuated the movements of the mohawk. He licked even harder. I came almost instantly; several wads of thick cum. The kid swallowed it all. Then he kissed me passionately and walked away into the crowd as quickly as he had arrived. All the while his mohawk was visible in the overhead red glow.

I moved toward the red exit light. I needed a nightcap at the bar. Thank God the friendly biker whom I met on the way in was still here. He still had his eyes glued to my butt. He nodded at me and slowly walked over. He smiled again. His brilliant white teeth were perfect. "So Miles, did you have a good time? Did they leave your gorgeous butt alone? Can I buy you a drink?" We talked for half an hour. I really liked him. I told him he was my Tom of Finland. He knew how to make me laugh. It was nearly closing time. Tom asked if I wanted a ride home on his Harley. "Only if you promise to make love to my butt and then hold me in your arms until sunrise." Tom chuckled. "It's a deal. Get onboard kid. You're making my head spin. My place or yours?"

7 / I STILL HAVE YOUR NUMBER

I was in the remote Montreal office for a couple of days. Normally Abbey would come along, but this time he had to be at a medical conference. It was the middle of February; bitterly cold. When I checked into the local Hilton I noticed the friendly guy at the concierge desk. He looked like he might be gay, super-cute and friendly. As he bent over to take my luggage I got a clear shot of his chinos. They were skin-tight and clearly showed off his swollen erection and his spectacular bubble butt. He saw me staring at them. I couldn't help myself. I felt the first thrill of arousal. He smiled as he gave himself a quick squeeze. His intent was unmistakable. He slipped me a hand written phone number on a hotel business card. I presumed it was his private number. Could he be a local hustler when he wasn't behind the concierge desk? I figured this guy would know if there were any gay bars near the hotel. When I asked him, he told me there weren't, but there was a gay bathhouse open 24/7 right around the corner that he frequented. I decided to give it a shot. "Care to join me at the baths this evening? My late afternoon flight left me extra horny. I'm Miles." "You bet. I get off at nine. I'm John. This cold weather gives me a hardon. Plus I'm overdue for a good spanking in case you're interested." "You have a sexy butt. I'm sure something can be arranged." So that's how I met the hotel's S&M hustler.

I showed up at the baths at 8:30 pm. It was an extremely cold night with crunchy Canadian snow on the ground. The baths' entrance was off the main street in a deserted alleyway. I could see a few fresh footsteps in the snow leading up to the entrance. Someone had recently cleared away the snow on the front steps. Once inside I felt as if I had arrived at some distant outpost in the Artic. I stomped my boots on the floor mat and stepped inside. The interior was tiny, much smaller than I expected. It looked empty. It was washed in an icy blue fog from the overhead fluorescent lights. A small check-in counter was shoved into one corner with a glass case full of condoms, lube and sex toys. I noticed a leather sex paddle that might come in handy later with John. There was no attendant. Opposite the check-in was a narrow staircase leading up to a small locker room and a wet sauna. The reddish glow from above was warm and inviting like an enticing entrance to queer heaven.

I heard light footsteps coming down the staircase. "Hello, hold on. I'm on my way. Just a minute." It was a young boyish attendant. He sounded flustered. I liked him immediately. He reminded me of myself, definitely a little ditsy. "Welcome. I see you braved the cold night. It must be thirty below." What a cute face. He was completely adorable. I hadn't seen such an attractive youthful face in days. Concierge John was equally youthful, but unlike this kid, John had the gritty edge of a seasoned street hustler. This kid's smile put me at ease. He was an angel. I told him I was from New York City, solo, expecting a young man from the Hilton soon for a little rough action in the steam room. I mentioned I'd probably need the sex paddle in the display case. He acted like that was to be expected. I asked for his best room. He chuckled and said the place was empty. "It's too cold out for the baths. It's just me holding down the fort. You can have room number six. It's our best. There's really no need to check you in. This is not exactly the Club Baths in New York City. Could I interest you in a soda or a cold beer while you wait for your friend? By the way, I'm Tony." "Nice to meet you. I'm Miles."

While waiting for John to show up I got a little acquainted with Tony. He was refreshingly candid. He told me he enjoys working at the baths because he gets plenty of sex on the side with strangers. He likes the variety. He's seen everything. He's strictly a bottom, always on the lookout for the perfect top. He even asked me if I'd like to fuck him. "You bet I would. You know you have a very sexy butt." "I'd really like that, but let's first see what your friend has in mind."

Concierge John arrived a little after nine with a blast of cold air and a flurry of fresh snow. Tony locked the front door and hung out the closed sign for the evening. It turned out John and Tony know each other well from the baths. When things are dead at the Hilton they often fool around here. When John saw me standing in the middle of the room he immediately stripped, dropping his chinos and pulling out his cock. I pounced on it immediately. I'd been dreaming of sucking him off all afternoon. His dick was as beautiful in the raw as when I'd seen it packaged inside his chinos. I blew him right then and there. He knew he was hot. He enjoyed showing off his six pack. He was an exhibitionist slapping his hard cock against my outstretched tongue. John obviously enjoyed playing the idol. I didn't care. I would gladly play his slut. I was famished for his cock. Tony watched the whole scene frozen in total silence.

With that pent-up introduction now out of the way, we stripped down and settled into the steam room for our orgy. By default I played the Master. John would be my slave and Tony would be my butt boy. John asked me for a spanking using the leather paddle from downstairs. He confessed he'd been a bad boy. During his last confession he fucked a horny priest inside the confessional. "I'm Catholic so I really need a spanking." I sensed he just made up the story. I think he just wanted me to spank him. So I really let him have it. The pops were loud and sharp. His butt cheeks turned bright red. I heard him moan in deepest pleasure. John really enjoyed the burn.

Then Tony made himself comfortable on the steam room bench with several giant cushions. His hairless butt was pure white, the dark crack was so inviting. He asked me to butt fuck him gently. "Pretend you are my father." I told him I'd love to and slipped on a condom. I went nice and slow with an ocean of love. When Tony announced he was about to cum I got so excited for him that I came at the same time. "Fuck me Daddy, fuck me." I must have cum a record. I'd been saving it up for weeks. The entire evening was perfect. An S&M hustler and a boy angel made an old man extremely happy on the coldest night of the year.

Afterwards we showered and left for Chinese food at a late-night diner.

John and Tony told me they never felt closer. They credited that to me. They thanked me for being their missing fathers. Relaxing over dinner, we traded our life stories. They both wanted to hear all about Stonewall and gay liberation. I told them about my crazy years in New York City after coming out. They were impressed with how long my first relationship with Jim lasted. I told them about the breakup and my searching for love in the leather bars and backrooms, until I finally found Abbey, the love of my life.

Tony grew up on a farm in Alberta. He loves the wide-open spaces and the wild horses. He has a younger brother who is also gay. They are very close. Tony tries to protect his brother from the things that hurt him while growing up gay with a homophobic father. He's not always successful but he knows his brother loves him for trying. Tony is working on a degree in nursing from McGill. He lives alone with his kitty. He's strictly a bottom. He spends most nights at the baths, more often than not he leaves lonely. He thanked me for taking good care of him. He gave me a long warm hug. He told me tonight's sex had changed his life forever. Finally he felt like a whole gay man.

John is a city boy. His father was a military man. They traveled all over the globe when John was growing up. His father was extremely strict. When he caught John having queer sex in a tearoom he whipped him with his leather belt. John never felt like he had a father growing up. He ran away to Montreal after high school. John also has a younger brother who is gay, but unlike Tony, John was never close to his gay brother. John is ambitious. He's working on his Master's degree in hotel administration. He wants to make a lot of money and wear fancy clothes. He wants to travel and see the world. He's both a top and a bottom. He's into S&M sex. He thanked me for the spanking. He told me he really enjoyed it. He wants to see me again before I leave Montreal, maybe at the baths. "Sure, you bet kid. I still have your number."

The three of us said goodbye at sunrise. It was close to minus forty. The huge plate glass window of the Chinese restaurant was covered in thin sheets of fractured ice like a giant snowflake. It was beautiful in the morning sunlight.

8 / MIDNIGHT PRAYER

The #1 New York City subway platform at Columbus Circle and West 59th Street was deserted at midnight. Well, not completely. My friend Keith Haring, the gay graffiti-inspired Pop artist was busy at the other end of the platform. He was preoccupied working on one of his black and white wall murals of gay men line dancing. Twisting white torsos with their arms in the air over their heads. It was really good. Keith was a genius. He had to work really fast so the graffiti cops didn't catch him. He worked late into the night after the gay clubs closed. Besides the subway projects like this, I'd see him around the West Village, mostly hanging out in the butch leather bars. He certainly was a nighthawk. It looked like he was already finished. He headed to the turnstile exit with his painting supplies. He waved goodbye.

The platform was dead quiet. I must have just missed the #1 downtown to the World Trade Center. I was headed home to my loft at Nassau and Fulton. I knew it would be at least forty-five minutes before the next train arrived. I was coming from the New York City Ballet at Lincoln Center. It was the last ticket from Jim and my subscriptions since we broke up nearly two months ago. Jim's already resettled in San Francisco with his new boyfriend Sandy. He has already moved on. Not me. I'm still a wreck. Actually, the only reason I even went to the ballet alone tonight was to drool over the cute male dancers in their white tights. They are always so attractive. That plus the butch guys in the audience showing off their black leather. Those two subgroups were often the best part of going to the ballet with Jim. He would never admit it, but I knew that was true. I always looked for the West Village homos in their black leather.

Tonight was a good example. There was this hot guy dressed in a biker's jacket with leather chaps over old Levi's. It was like something straight out of the Mine Shaft. He was posing alone at the downstairs bar during the intermissions. We made eye contact numerous times. This guy was especially hot. His leather chaps were tight around his cute butt. He turned to show me the whole package. Just the way I like it. He looked like he was plenty interested. He even followed me into the men's toilet on the Dress Circle. We had a little private showing at the urinal trough. His cock was Major League. All this was just my pathetic attempt to prove to myself that my shattered sex life following Jim's departure was still somehow intact. As if I could still pick-up ballet leather queens at the New York City Ballet. Sure, just like in the old days. I only wish right? I'm pathetic. So here I am all alone on the number one platform at one in the morning waiting for the fucking subway. I'm really so pathetic.

The platform was still deserted. I was getting a little nervous. You hear about people in New York City being mugged or murdered on deserted subway platforms late at night. It happens all the time. They never report it; they're afraid it will spook the tourists. When Jim and I did the ballet at Lincoln Center together years ago it seemed a whole lot safer. I probably should have stayed at home tonight or at least taken a cab. Suddenly I heard the after-hours entry turnstile to the platform at the other end of the station. I thought of Keith, but he was long gone. My heart skipped a beat. This could be serious trouble, perhaps even a mugger. To my complete surprise, it was the hot guy from the Dress Circle men's toilet. I recognized the sexy leather chaps.

He smiled at me. I guess he must have followed me from Lincoln Center. He must be headed home to Greenwich Village. Nodding friendly-like, he started walking toward me. I freaked out. I froze. I didn't want to do anything that might encourage his attention. But he just kept walking toward me slowly. Then all of a sudden he disappeared into the subway men's room just twenty feet in front of me. I was stunned. I should have seen this coming.

40

After all he had followed me earlier into the Dress Circle men's room. This time he left the door ajar. He must be a tearoom queen. I could hear my heart pounding. Should I go in after him? I didn't hesitate more than a moment. I was definitely all in. I recalled his large cock dangling over the urinal trough. It was gorgeous, long and thick. I imagined sucking him off with my eyes closed. I slowly pushed the door open. I took the plunge and stepped inside. The men's room was small with only two stalls. He was standing alone in the middle facing the door.

"Hi, I'm Jeffery." "I'm Miles." Seeing him up close face-to-face for the first time I was embarrassed. He looked so relaxed and comfortable. I sensed he must have been here before. I was just the opposite; I was a total wreck. With an outstretched hand meant to calm me, he offered me his open popper bottle. I took one hit. It did the trick. I relaxed as my whole head exploded. I felt warm. I could feel my cock stiffen. I automatically dropped down on my knees in front of him in total adoration. He opened his button fly and dropped the chaps and Levi's to the floor. Then he handed me his erection. It was magnificent. I licked the shaft from the base to the tip, then swallowed it whole in one pass. Jeffery looked down admiring his cock as it slid in and out of my mouth. He groaned softly.

This guy was straight out of an erotic dream. I was in queer heaven. It was nearly two months since I had made love to a gay man. I was famished. I took everything Jeffery had to offer. "What a cock." I slid my hands around his upper thighs squeezing the plump butt cheeks hard. I had been wanting to do this since I'd seen him standing at the bar. I slid my fingers into the butt crack, rubbing its length up and down over and over. I could do this forever. The leatherman spoke. "Please fuck me. I can tell you want to." "Yes I do Jeffery, but not here. Let me make love to you in my bed." I craved this exchange more than he'd ever know. It would be my first queer sex in many weeks since my breakup with Jim. I cried. I felt tremendous gratitude toward Jeffery as he held me close like a protective father. We caught the number one to the World Trade Center. I took Jeffery to my loft nearby, to my bed, to the bed Jim and I made love in for nine years.

We lost all sense of time. Jeffery and I made queer love in my bed until daybreak. Jeffery knew it meant the world to me. He just wanted to see me happy. He seemed to understand exactly what I'd been through recently. His own story was not all that different. Six months ago Jeffery's boyfriend left him for a twenty-something twinkie. Our shared intimacy that night was the most healing sex I've ever shared with another gay man. It was deeply personal. We both knew it was only meant to be on this single night. It was a bittersweet glimpse into a private haven reserved for two shy gay men. Our bond that night formed a sacred prayer.

9 / Night's Calling

It served Robbie well as his nightly escape, his nightly calling, soothing like a soft blanket from his childhood, always something he could count on. It was his connection to the beautiful men he worshipped, those butch queers who practiced outlaw sex each night inside the infamous Ramble. The 38-acre forested landscape was anything but natural. It was a contrived queer's paradise. The rugged grounds were overgrown, crisscrossed by dirt paths to serve as New York City's largest gay cruising grounds, an outdoor sex playground of pleasure. Robbie knew it well, each crest and valley, each twist and turn. He had long ago memorized the more visible gathering spots popular with the closeted tourists looking for a cheap sexual thrill away from the wife. But lately Robbie was more drawn to the secluded hidden paths tinged with danger, frequented by the hardcore sexual nighthawks in their black leather biker jackets, their leather chaps, their studded harnesses. This was where Robbie found real satisfaction, where he found the night's true calling.

When it came time to really settle into New York City, to claim his own turf, Robbie made sure he ended up living on Central Park West only a block away from the main Ramble entrance. It was convenient to his nightly outings, whether long or short, depending on the season of the year or the night's weather. Afterwards, Robbie would frequently invite his partners back to his apartment, to relax, to clean up, to share a story, a beer, make a new friend. Robbie always bonded with these men. They formed his brotherhood. He rarely included his live-in lover George who never really understood, who was always critical, too square. Robbie was secretly glad George had to travel frequently for his work. Over the years the Ramble became Robbie's private world, not to be shared with George. It was where he met the queer outlaws Robbie most admired.

I asked Robbie to introduce me to his world, to a few of his closest buddies, to a few of the hunting spots he enjoyed the most. I certainly didn't want to intrude, to play voyeur, to upset the delicate balance. Robbie gave it careful thought. He suggested I meet his close buddy Colton, a softcore leatherman who had moved to New York City a year ago and was looking for new friendships. Robbie knew from personal experience that Colton was well-endowed and really into queer butt sex. Robbie was sure I'd have a good time. Plus Colton is super-friendly and thoughtful. He's a nightly regular in the Ramble so he'd be the perfect guide. Robbie suggested first a trial run between just Colton and me in the heart of the Ramble. If that rendezvous went well, Robbie and Abbey could join in. Robbie wanted me to experience the hunt, the thrill of a new sexual encounter with Colton.

I showed up after midnight at Colton's favorite cruising spot. As Robbie predicted, he was posing alone next to an enormous boulder. He was in a studded leather harness and leather chaps over bare flesh. His butt inside the chaps was spectacular. It looked like those Tom of Finland butts, plump round orbs, soft and full, just begging to be touched.

He turned so I could see the cheeks in the full moon, especially the deep butt crack that I found so intoxicating. He must have seen me approaching his backside on the right very slowly, but he didn't move an inch. He just waited patiently like a seasoned fisherman slowly reeling in his catch. I remembered Robbie's comment that Colton is a butt sex queen. I was in for a treat. I boldly touched his right butt cheek giving it the slightest squeeze. It was totally thrilling. I spit out a wad of saliva on my fingers and placed it deep in his butthole with my middle finger. He smiled. "You must be Miles." "Yes Sir." I gently pressed in two more fingers, twisting them together as a bundle. "Hello Colton. Your butt is super-hot. May I rim you?" "Sure, but once you start you'll have to finish the job." We did just that taking turns butt fucking

44

into the night. With rosy butts and spent cocks, we screwed tight up against the massive boulder. Colton liked to play rough, nice and slow; he knew how to please me. We climaxed together, jerking each other off, our loads of cum thick and heavy.

Back at Robbie's apartment we shared all the details with Robbie and Abbey. Colton had everyone rolling on the floor. Colton was adorable; he won me over with his first smile. I really liked him. Beside his stunning butt Colton had a great sense of humor and told the best dirty jokes that got Abbey shedding tears. So our first encounter went off perfectly as planned. We became casual sex buddies. Thanks to Colton and Robbie, Abbey and I soon learned our way around the Ramble. They showed us their favorite cruising spots. Robbie always looked after us closely like a protective father. When George was away on bank business Abbey and I would sometimes sleep over. We'd cruise the Ramble together, having sex with horny strangers. Robbie's a voyeur like me so sometimes we'd just watch from the sidelines trading notes afterwards.

The three of us would always end up snuggling in Robbie's big bed. That was the best part. His bedroom had an enormous window overlooking Central Park. Robbie never put a shade on that window. The view in the fall was spectacular. The apartment was only on the second floor so we mostly looked at the towering trees. It was the most beautiful after a fresh wet snowfall in winter, all the branches outlined in white. We'd hold on to each other all night staring at the yellow taxicabs with their red taillights gliding past the window. We'd take turns giving each other slow blowjobs. Robbie had the most perfectly proportioned cock. Robbie was my second prince after Abbey. Within six years, Robbie died of AIDS. I still miss him. We never saw George after that. We heard through a mutual friend that George hung himself, drunk, hurling himself over the side of his sailboat in a marina in the Bahamas, discovered dead days later. What a total waste. George never understood Robbie. He never joined the queer brotherhood. He never joined in the dance. A miserable isolated soul, George died a lonely death.

After Robbie died, Abbey and I went back to the Ramble only once. We were on a sacred mission. Robbie had asked us to scatter his ashes in the Ramble on a moonlit night. It was a beautiful warm spring evening; the apple trees were still full of their white blossoms. I wept like a baby as I fulfilled Robbie's last request. Afterwards, Abbey and I watched for hours from Colton's favorite boulder. It was all so peaceful; the silent parade of those queer men of different ages, of all creeds and colors; performing the ancient sex rituals of the night's calling; their stiff shiny cocks glowing proudly in the moonlight.

10 / A Good Distraction

It was a rainy Tuesday evening. I was walking home from the West Village to my loft near City Hall. I'd struck out again in the leather bars. No surprise. It has been months since Jim and I broke up. I was feeling a little depressed. I decided to walk through Soho on the way home. The shop windows are a good distraction. It was already getting dark. The galleries and shops were closing up for the night. The metal window grates always made a huge racket as they came crashing down to the ground. The streets in Soho were deserted. At Spring Street I saw some commotion up ahead. It looked like a couple of bikers with their motorcycles. They were standing outside an unmarked metal door in the drizzle. These guys sure looked butch. They could take the rain. Not like me, the sissy with the Briggs umbrella. The top floor windows of the four-story building were all lit up. It was one of those beautiful white cast-iron loft buildings with huge arched windows. The ones famous artists like Donald Judd live in. It looked like someone was throwing a huge party tonight. As I got closer I recognized the two bikers. It was Jack and Gerhard from the Ramrod. I know them slightly. They're a biracial leather couple. I'd seen them in the bar earlier this evening. "Hey Miles. Are you headed upstairs?" I didn't understand. Gerhard explained. "It's a party for New York Jacks the J.O. club. You should join us. We're members. You can be our guest." Looking up from the sidewalk across the street I could see men posing in the windows. I thought I saw a nude blond guy walk past an open window. I wanted to go upstairs to see if I could find him.

So we all rode up in the giant freight elevator, along with the two black and chrome Harleys. The elevator opened directly into the huge loft. It was well lit and crowded with several dozen guys milling about mostly silent. It was incredible; most guys were buck naked engaged in heavy J.O. sex in pairs or circle jerks. Gerhard told me the club dates back to 1980. That's when Jack and he joined. Once inside I checked in with the cute attendant. He made me feel welcome so I joined the club on the spot. I stripped down to my work boots, checked my clothes and grabbed a small paper cup of special lube. All the while I kept an eye out for the blond guy I'd seen from the street. Sure enough, I spotted him in a corner. I was in luck. He was all alone. I walked over and introduced myself while casually placing my hand on his greased erection. Since he immediately smiled, I gathered that was considered proper etiquette. His name was Stanley. He had an English accent. He followed my lead, greasing me up with lube and started stroking my cock nice and slow the way I like it. It was outrageous. He was clearly a J.O. pro. We made chit-chat as if we were on line for a midnight movie at the Quad. It really was a turn-on pretending to be so nonchalant while having J.O. sex out in the open. Stanley worked my whole shaft perfectly with just one hand without even looking down once. He just looked at my face the whole time to see if I was happy.

Then just when I thought he was finished, Stanley surprised me with his free hand on my butt. "Would you be interested in giving me a spanking?" Before I could reply he handed me his leather paddle. It was thick and heavy. Stanley spoke again, more to the point. "I noticed you were staring at my butt." "Indeed I was. You sure picked the right guy to give you a spanking. I'd love to. Show me your butt." It was beautiful. The pale butt cheeks resembled a pair of smooth melons ready for a master's touch. His dark butt crack was driving me crazy. I started off gentle and slow. The loud sharp pops were a real turn-on. Our spanking attracted a circle jerk around us. I enjoyed playing the exhibitionist for a change. Stanley asked me to slap him even harder. That was no problem; I happily obliged. The pink flesh turned bright red. He winced with each slap while moaning out loud. When his spanking was finally over, I grabbed his stiff hardon and jerked him off in classic J.O. style. His cock head exploded in my hand as I milked the glans hard. He released a shower of cum. He practically collapsed in my arms. Afterwards we took it easy. I showed him the city landmarks from the enormous loft windows. It turned out Stanley was an English tourist traveling on his own, checking out the hottest sex spots in New York City. He told me New York Jacks was at the top of his list.

Thankfully New York Jacks is still around today. It is still very active. It has a dedicated following with over three hundred members. For many of these guys, New York Jacks is the core of their sex lives. If you follow their rules, it's completely safe and also plenty of fun. I've always admired the club's matter-of-factness. We are all there for one purpose only; just to indulge in pure J.O. sex. When you walk through the door your cock belongs to everyone so be prepared to share it with your brothers. Give your partner the ride of his life. Don't forget, this is J.O. sex, plain and simple. Leave your ego down on the street.

11 / Snowy Night

The ad in the *New York Native* for Man's Country read "ten floors of fantasy." The Manhattan gay bathhouse on West 15th Street occupied ten floors with twenty-six private rooms. It was a tall slender building. Perhaps that was to encourage men to stay in shape by climbing the stairs. It worked. The club had a world-wide reputation for gorgeous men wrapped in skimpy white towels. The fantasies on the other hand varied widely. There was your usual locker room and the always popular steam room, plus a truck stop, jail cell, orgy room, gym and Jacuzzi. The restaurant called Meet Rack was hardly Lutece. Where it really stood out was as a concert venue with its stage for live performers. Not just tired old drag queens, but the likes of the New York Dolls, Boy George, the Village People, Grace Jones, Charles Pierce, Bette Midler and the heart-throb Barry Manilow. Midler was famous for tossing tiny popper bottles out to her adoring fans. Long before I met my true love Abbey, he dated Manilow for a month or two. He broke my Abbey's heart. But Abbey found better sex partners upstairs with the hot Porto Rican kids than downstairs on the stage with Barry crooning Broadway showtunes on a baby grand.

Snow at night in Central Park is so romantic. The noisy city is actually quiet for a change. The sky turns a pearly cream color. Everyone comes out of their tiny apartments to see the magical snow. The city never looked so clean. Strangers are actually friendly. They even take time out to greet each other.

Some make snow angels; others throw snow balls or ride in a horse-drawn sled. That's when I think back on Jerry, my trick from Man's Country. Jerry was special.

I was home all alone. It was a snowy night. I decided I'd go to the baths. Man's Country would fit the bill nicely. I was looking for something a little raunchy. The place was moderately crowded. I started cruising the halls, taking the elevator to the top floor working my way down. On floor eight I passed a gorgeous Black stud cruising naked with the most handsome butt imaginable. He must have caught me staring at it. "Like what you see?" "You have a butt from heaven." Without speaking another word, he grabbed my hand and took us to a private toilet locking the door. He leaned over the sink, his muscular arms on the porcelain. "Fuck me hard." I was caught totally off guard. "Excuse me?" "I said fuck me hard." "Okay, you got it." So I delivered. It was incredible. One for the record books. Afterwards we shared a beer at the bar. He had just broken up with a twinkie boyfriend whom he caught cheating on him in their bed. Getting fucked by a total stranger who appreciated him made him feel a whole lot better. He asked me back to his room for another round of butt sex, this time in bed. "Go ahead Miles, please fuck me again, this time slowly with love." I must have been at it for half an hour. I made love to his beautiful butt—kissing the cheeks, licking the crack. I simply couldn't get enough. What a beautiful man. Afterwards we checked out and went for a long walk in Central Park to see the freshly fallen snow. The city was hushed and still. We exchanged numbers but I never called Jerry. It was meant to be a one-night stand. Now whenever I walk in Central Park on a snowy night I think of Jerry and his beautiful derriere. It always makes me smile.

Years later on another snowy night I returned to Man's Country. It wasn't like I remembered. To my surprise the stage and piano were gone. No sign of the performers. Instead, it had been turned into a hardcore gay sex club. The men were less friendly, raw and impatient. Since I'd already paid my admission fee, I decided to check it out.

On level five I hit bingo. A door was left slightly ajar. Inside a brown-skinned

Porto Rican teenager was half asleep on a white towel, his head of curls on a white pillow. His gorgeous butt was fully exposed. We made long eye contact. He nodded and invited me in. He had carefully arranged a popper bottle, a condom and a small tube of KY next to his ass. He had me fully aroused. He turned to check me out. "I'm Jose. I usually only let younger guys fuck me. But you can fuck me for a hundred dollars if you use a condom."

His blunt demand reminded me of my first brief encounter with Jerry in the hallway. Both felt like sex on demand. I decided to teach young Jose a lesson. I gave him his money. Then I slipped on the condom and lubed up. I fucked his tight pretty ass long and hard to kingdom come. He wailed like a baby. "In the future you should show your elders a little more respect. One day you'll be a horny old man like me."

Years later Abbey and I had subscriptions to the Sunday afternoon piano recitals at Carnegie Hall. We always enjoyed them immensely. During intermission I ran into Jerry at the downstairs bar. He actually remembered my name. I introduced him to Abbey. We all had a hearty good laugh. Years earlier I had told Abbey all about my magical snowy night of butt sex with Jerry in Man's Country. I immediately recalled Jerry's gorgeous butt crack. Jerry introduced us to his husband Jose, a stunning Porto Rican dancer.

Jose put it all together. He remembered the snowy night back in Man's Country when I taught him a lesson in love. Jose gave me a warm hug. "Thank you Miles. You helped me when I really needed it the most. You taught me an important lesson that night. You helped me find my beloved Jerry." The four of us had a group hug. I closed my eyes and recalled Jerry and Jose's beautiful butt cracks from years ago, still so soft and erotic in my mind's eye. I could still picture them perfectly, each so plump and round. I was fully aroused in an instant. Jerry smiled. "Go ahead Miles, have a squeeze behind the curtain. You know you want to." So I ran my fingers up and down the outer seams in the back of their trousers nice and slow. I was transported back to Man's Country. "Thank you boys. I always dream of doing that whenever it snows in Central Park at night." Jose chuckled. "You're an amazing old man Miles, you're a romantic."

12 / WHEN
YOU'RE READY

I was doing a little overtime in the office. The place was totally empty. It was a late winter afternoon with a light rain. I knew the pier would only be busy for a few more hours. This was when the hardcore outlaws showed up in their black leather jackets for S&M sex. These were the guys who got off on danger, the thrill of anonymous sex with strangers inside the abandoned pier. I felt the erotic charge take hold, pulling me under its spell. I'd been stiff all afternoon, my hardon straining tight inside my Levi's. It was 2:30 pm. That was enough work for the day. Finally I was off. I zipped up my motorcycle jacket as I hailed a cab on Park Avenue. "Pier Fifty-two." The cabbie put it all together immediately. His face was weathered and wise. "I like your old leather jacket. You look like Marlon Brando in "The Wild One." With this rain the pier should be hopping." "That's the idea. You look pretty hot yourself. Robert De Niro in "Taxi Driver." Maybe I'll catch you inside the Pier later. I'm Miles." The cabbie smiled with a nod as he pulled away from the curb. "I'm Jax."

Walking away I saw the enormous hulk of the ruined pier through the bare branches of the trees at the end of Gansevoort Street. It still looked spectacular. The same industrial ruin I had first admired years before, still abandoned and dilapidated, its erotic secrets hidden away inside. Its huge rectangular form was still jutting out proudly into the Hudson River like an enormous ruined pleasure palace.

I was always drawn to Pier 52, New York City's infamous "sex pier." It appealed to the closeted sexual outlaw in me. Jim was my initial guide on several occasions years ago, long before our breakup. But those limited tours of the West Village landmark only covered the building's vast crumbling exterior. As two timid voyeurs, we always kept a safe distance, we never dared to venture inside. Rather, we stared up in awe at the beautiful shirtless men hanging out at decayed windows on the upper floors, some walking around nude with semi-erections and most memorable of all, some brazen exhibitionists performing live sex acts out in the open for all to see, free of charge.

Now, when I returned years later to Pier 52, I was on my own, seeking out a little closure. Jim had died of AIDS a year before. This Sunday I vowed to return and to go inside. It would mark my first solo visit. How appropriate that it was a Sunday, for the open cavernous interior felt much like a cathedral. It lived up to its hallowed reputation. Huge interior spaces in total ruin, hushed tones of reverence, dangerous cat walks, men cruising men everywhere, lots of black leather, lots of kinky sex, lots of nudity, more sex, in fact, sex at every turn.

Before leaving I went to a much smaller, more secluded room, one of the cathedral's side chapels. There was no door, just two extremely tall narrow openings in opposite corners. Just like in a church, anyone could wander through, stay for as long as they wished. It was lit by a single overhead shaft of light which filled the otherwise dark interior. The light reached down into the middle of the room, where it illuminated a free-standing raised platform, which held a large rusty old bedframe and an abandoned used mattress.

A towering shirtless Atlas, an obvious handsome body builder, dressed only in work boots and black Levi's, was looking down at the mattress, intensely focused on his lover, his butt boy, a naked much younger man lying on his stomach, his beautiful white butt fully exposed, his hands and feet already tied with heavy soft ropes to the four corners of the bed frame.

It was a fisting den. I was fascinated and frightened at the same time. The Master leaned over his lover's beautiful prize, squeezing the melons hard, slapping the plump orbs with his bare hands, then again with his thick leather belt. After a long time lost in a trance, the Master turned away to dip his tightly closed fist into a large open can of Crisco, smearing the creamy white grease on his fist and up his forearm, working it in slowly, rubbing it in again and again. I knew where this was headed. The Master carefully positioned the fist at the anus opening. He applied the gentlest pressure. I heard long moans of pain, of release and then of pure pleasure. I gasped as the Master continued, determined, resolute, driven by his lustful desire.

I surprised myself and stayed for it all. I wasn't the only one in attendance. Half a dozen bikers had showed up as well. I paired up with the one wearing a black leather codpiece. It captured my full attention. It was my perfect escape. The black convex surface was shiny. There were two silver snap buttons on each side. The biker noticed my fixed stare. He smiled. I boldly placed my hand on the warm leather pouch. He nodded placing his hand over mine giving it a firm squeeze. I could feel his cock jump and stiffen. My mouth went completely dry.

He snapped open the top two buttons. The biker's hardon was finally free, hanging out proudly for all to admire. It was thick and long. The tip was wet with pre-cum. I instantly swallowed it whole. The biker was lost looking up at the ceiling, at the skylight filled with the red clouds of dusk. The Master was mesmerized by the dramatic blowjob at sunset. He passed me his popper bottle. My head exploded. I watched the Master slowly approach me. He whispered in my ear. "So you want to get fisted tonight kid?" "Only in my dreams Sir. I'm a sissy." I turned to face the Master squarely. I wanted to show him my full respect. He smiled. He rubbed my head gently mussing the hair down to my shoulders. "You're new here aren't you kid? I'm sure you'll be back. I'll be here when you're ready."

As I left the pier stepping out into the drizzle I noticed the red sky had lost all its color. I saw a yellow taxicab parked on West Street. A cabbie was waiting inside; his window was down as he took a drag on his cigarette. I noticed his old motorcycle jacket with its worn epilates and dull silver studs. I figured he was looking for a leathermen leaving the pier at nightfall. When he turned to face me frontally, I recognized his weathered face. It was beautiful. It was Jax. I smiled. "Hey Jax buddy, you came after all. Thank you. I could really use some company tonight." "Hello Miles. Jump in kid. Shall we hit the Empire Diner? You look like you need a hug."

13 / VISITATION

It was well past one am. I was feeling a little restless. I couldn't sleep. Abbey was away on business for an AmFAR conference in L A. I missed him. I pulled his pillow over my nose. The strong smell of him made my head spin. I took in a few more deep breaths. I really missed him. I recalled the touch of his backside which I love so much—his head of soft curls, the small soft ears that were somehow always warm, the plump inviting butt cheeks I loved to squeeze and slap while we were making love and most of all the butt crack which always gives me an erection.

Turning on my back in the middle of the huge bed, I closed my eyes and felt the thrill of arousal wash over me; the subtle hint of a stiffening cock. My J.O. sessions are always lengthy, but with Abbey gone they seemed even longer. I put on my favorite queer porno and reached for the lube. I added a few extra drops and then jerked-off nice and slow. The bed sheets will definitely need a changing. The wads of white cum were everywhere.

I lay still for a long time taking it all in. I was finally completely relaxed. I walked over to the open window to take in the city view. It was a beautiful clear night. The moon was out and full. The city was fast asleep. I was standing naked at one of the huge double-hung loft windows facing east. The night sky was filled with a thousand stars high above the city's skyscrapers. As my eyes scanned the heavens, I was reminded how insignificant we are. Mere specks, if even that.

Quiet Nassau Street far below me was totally deserted. I must have been the only person looking out a window in all of New York's Financial District. I realized I was standing nude, visible from the street in the full moon. A city garbage truck below passed by our windows. It stopped abruptly at the corner. The giant guy in a bright orange suit stepped off the truck bumper step. In one graceful movement, he emptied the trash can into the open bin at the back of the truck. He looked like a God. The compressor made a loud heaving sound as the massive truck pulled away to the next corner. The worker nodded as he spotted me naked up in the window.

That's when I first noticed the lad. He looked like a white angel. Was he real or just a vision of my imagination? I was smitten from the first moment I saw him. He was standing perfectly still all alone under the lamp post at the corner of Nassau and Fulton. He oddly looked like he was out for a midnight stroll, surely just a sweet teenager, too neat to be homeless, too innocent to be a street hustler. His curly black hair was half way down to his buttocks. He was dressed in gray painter's overalls with a white Yankees baseball cap. Underneath the dirty overalls was a pink cotton t-shirt. The moon turned the pink into the only patch of color in the streetscape of gray on gray.

Could this be his maiden voyage? He looked so innocent. Could he be a young nighthawk cruising the empty streets in the wee hours for the first time? I felt my exposed cock stiffen. His painter's overalls were ripe with desire. He was definitely looking up at my window. He was staring at my cock. Our eyes locked for a long time; then he turned to walk away. I was crestfallen. I was deeply disappointed. What a wasted opportunity. I turned to close the window. Wait, hold it, not so fast. I was mistaken. I smiled. I was saved. He was just turning to show me his backside. My night visitor was a peacock in heat. He lowered the overalls to reveal a pair of plump butt cheeks. They glowed pale white in the moonlight. He somehow knew I would be most interested in these. I wanted to make love to him right then and there in the street standing tall and proud; to gently caress his butt cheeks, to lick the butt crack, to rim his virgin anus. I wanted to fuck this boy angel. He looked up at me coyly as if that was exactly his plan. He walked over slowly standing below my window. My night visitor was eager to meet.

I put my door keys inside an old sock, rolled them in a tight ball and tossed them out the window. I waited patiently at the open window taking in the cool night air. A minute passed. Then another. Finally I heard the door buzzer ring in my kitchen. I loudly spoke my loft number into the speaker, cracked open the front door and waited off to the side. I heard the hum of the elevator. The elevator cab jolted to an abrupt stop. I waited. A lengthy silence followed, then the door opened slowly. Suddenly the lad himself was standing just a few feet in front of me. He was gorgeous.

Neither of us dared to break the silence. He smiled as I slowly undressed him, taking away one piece of clothing at a time. He wore an old jockstrap under the overalls. I removed it with my teeth and swallowed his cock whole in one pass. This had to be a dream. It was just too perfect. We were hungry lovers trading meaty blowjobs. I fucked him hard in my shower under the hot water. He was standing tall in a corner, his arms raised high above his head just like Saint Sebastian. He took each new position in silently. I spared him nothing. I figured this would be the lad's education. He responded with adulation. He just wanted to please his teacher. Afterwards I wrapped him in a white towel kissing his black curls. He hardly spoke a word. His broken English was adorable. He told me he was Italian. His name was Angelo. He was from Rome, in New York City on a brief vacation. He was out solo tonight looking at the empty city in the moonlight. He's an architecture student. We napped in Abbey and my bed. I took him to the Stage Diner on Nassau Street for an early breakfast. The city was slowly coming to life. Our moment of magic was over.

When Abbey returned the following day, I told him the whole story. He wanted to meet Angelo, maybe have a threesome. But Angelo had already left New York, off to Chicago; I'd probably never see him again. I guess there's a chance we'll see each other in Rome. Angelo gave me his Rome address. He lives in my dreams forever. The tall pale lad with the plump butt cheeks, the sweet boy with the tender anus. He had appeared out of the darkness like magic. I had fucked him until dawn in my shower, his arms raised high, silver beads of warm water running downward over his head of black curls, down the backside of his slender torso, down his gorgeous buttocks into the deep butt crack that left me completely dizzy.

14 / NIGHTHAWKS

It was just after one in the morning, a sight in the moonlight, the enormous brick vaults that formed the base of the soaring Brooklyn Bridge as it touched down to bedrock in Manhattan. The slender vaults were tall and graceful, as if the enormous weight of the bridge were nothing to bear. It always reminded me of the ancient Baths of Caracalla in Rome. Both were extraordinary feats of engineering. The full moon reflected off the choppy whitecaps of the East River illuminating the underside of the massive vaults in a continuous dance of light. As I admired the engineer Roebling's work, I took in the steady hum of automobile wheels on the open steel grating some eighty feet above my head. The automobile passengers were blind to the hidden world below them. It was a murky world of beefy musclemen with their boy toys. These were the men who practiced the ancient rituals of queer sex out in the open. They were all bold exhibitionists. These weren't the sissy mama's boys asleep in their cushy beds, the uptown faggots with their diamond gold rings. Rather these were the butch Leathermen into black leather, rough sex and kinky pleasure. Their moans went out unheeded; they were hidden in the darkness.

I was hanging out with my biker brothers until my Master arrived. He's not due until three am. My fellow nighthawks are sex-obsessed men looking for something forbidden late into the night. It's actually quite beautiful in the moonlight, their naked muscular bodies turning silver in the dance: silver shaved heads, silver torsos, silver buttocks, and silver cocks. So beautiful, these interlocking dancers in the moonlight: cocksuckers, butt fuckers, butt boys and boy toys. Leathermen fucking brazenly in the moonlight, their rent boys more than eager to please in the cool night breeze.

I could hear their heavy breathing, their soft moans of deepest pleasure, the sharp pops from spankings that made me smile. It was all hidden under the overhead hum, inaudible inside the shiny black limousines high overhead with their stern gentlemen in tuxedoes and their tinkling ladies in fur wraps, heading home to Brooklyn after a night spent at the Metropolitan Opera. They will never hear my world, nor see my vision of queer heaven. It's only meant for us nighthawks, those sex-obsessed men I love.

I am still waiting for my Master. It's busy tonight, many nighthawks in the shadows searching for connection. I can feel the sexual electricity; my cock is already erect. I'm in my leather jacket, bare chested with just a jockstrap and work boots. Nothing more is necessary. I'm ready for my Master. I'm in the deep recesses of the bridge, in these underground chambers. I sense other nighthawks hidden in the shadows. I can feel their presence.

I detect a stranger kneeling at my feet. I can hear his heavy breathing. I touch his smooth bald head. I can feel his soft touch on the backside of my thighs. He slides his hands up my legs to the buttocks, squeezing my soft butt cheeks under the elastic straps. I can feel his warm breath inside my jockstrap, his tongue on the elastic pouch, his warm mouth surrounding my balls in a flood of warm saliva. My cock swells tight inside the strap aching for release. At last the stranger pulls the jockstrap down and gorges on my wet cock. I'm overwhelmed. The stranger's mouth is warm and wet. He knows how to handle cock. His massive tongue first works the frenulum, taking in each fold. I'm in heaven but I mustn't cum yet. Not yet. My Master is due soon. But I can't help myself. The stranger has me captive. I indulge this skilled cocksucker for a minute, then a minute longer. His touch is so intoxicating. He demands immediate satisfaction. He sucks even harder. My cock head swells rock-hard in anticipation. I can't help myself. I lust for more. I fondle his mustache as the cock shaft glides down his throat. My body spasms as I release a sea of cum to be followed by another. He swallows them both as if he's totally famished. Elated, but exhausted, I slowly pull away. I kiss the top of his bald head; his skin is wet with sweat. The silent stranger vanishes into the shadows. I feel my Master's calling. I must leave. My hardon quickly softens. I tuck the limp cock safely in the jockstrap and return to my brothers preening in the moonlight.

Far off in the distance I can hear his motorcycle, the black and chrome Harley. He is near. I am excited. He didn't forget. I smile. I'm obsessed with Black men, with their beautiful plump butts, their massive black cocks. Soon I will feel my Master's black cock up my butt. He will make me feel alive.

Master has arrived. He's a biker dressed in black leather head to toe, sapphire baby blues, clean-shaven, his head of thick black hair is curly in the moonlight. He's posing next to the Harley, his codpiece front and center. He's my beautiful Black biker. As I unzip my leather jacket, I step out of the shadows into the blinding moonlight. My buttocks and jockstrap are brilliant white in the full moon. I turn to show him the butt crack. He nods to me in approval.

We have been here before, under these enormous vaults, adoring white ass and Black dick. "So you want me to make love to you again?" "Yes Master. I'm your butt boy." Without hesitating a moment, Master unsnapped his codpiece and revealed his mighty cock. I knelt down as he fed it down my throat. I could suck this cock till daybreak. Finally pulling away Master placed my torso over the Harley seat cushion, slipped on a condom and fucked me in the moonlight. Our love is so plain and simple, cock to butt, butt to cock. Releasing a loud wail to gay heaven, he shot his load up my ass again and then again. We are two jubilant queer nighthawks, made one by lust and desire. Male to male. Hidden, always hidden in the darkness. Oily skin and salty sweat, wet cocks and soft balls, thick wads of creamy cum. And steady overhead, the hum of shiny black limousines in the night.

www.ingramcontent.com/pod-product-compliance
Lightning Source LLC
Chambersburg PA
CBHW010729270326
41930CB00018B/3420